Dreams Alive:
Prayers by Teenagers

Dreams Alive: Prayers by Teenagers

Edited by

Carl Koch, FSC

Saint Mary's Press
Christian Brothers Publications
Winona, Minnesota

The publishing team included Carl Koch, FSC, development editor; Cheryl Drivdahl, copy editor; Barbara Bartelson, production editor and typesetter; Carolyn St. George, cover designer; pre-press, printing, and binding by the graphics division of Saint Mary's Press.

Printed in the United States of America

Printing: 6 5 4 3 2 1

Year: 1996 95 94 93 92 91

ISBN 0-88489-262-X

Contents

Preface

The prayers in this book touch on themes and feelings at the heart of teenagers' experience: the challenge of making important decisions, wonderment at creation, concern about the future of the environment, thanksgiving for friends, and so on. Students from Maine to Hawaii and Montana to Florida contributed to this collection. The prayers are honest and articulate. Some radiate optimism, some cast doubts. They reflect the depth of insight often overlooked in teenagers and also reveal the humor with which teenagers cope.

Gathering the Prayers

Much of the motivation for compiling this text came from educators who, upon visiting with the Saint Mary's Press staff, would ask if we had a book of prayers to use with youth groups, high school classes, youth retreats, or other programs for teenagers. These requests persisted. Finally, when I proposed that we publish a book of prayers for teenagers, the staff agreed and also recommended that the prayers should be written by teenagers themselves.

Consequently, in November 1989, I sent out a letter to all religious education chairpersons in Catholic high schools and parish religious education programs throughout the United States, inviting them to collect prayers and reflections of their students. The letter read: "The topics

the students choose to write about can be virtually anything that deals with concerns or themes of high interest
to young people. The selections may be funny or serious,
focused on themselves as individuals or on other people,
perhaps even reactions to national or world affairs. Most
important, we are looking for writing that reflects honesty, authenticity, and an awareness of the real world of
young people." I believe you will find that the prayers we
selected have all these qualities.

To ensure spontaneity, I asked that the students not
be told the prayers were being written for possible publi-
cation. Because many teachers ask students to write
prayers and reflections as a regular part of their class,
following this request presented no problems. When
teachers had selected prayers for submission, the writers
were given the opportunity to attach their full name,
initials, or first name, or to remain anonymous. All the
prayers were identified by the school or parish from
which they came.

By 15 May 1990, the stack of prayers I had received
looked about a foot high. The sheer number, the quality,
and the diversity stunned me. I began reading, sorting,
and selecting, but by the end of the summer, I still had
nearly three hundred typewritten pages of prayers that
had made it through the first cut. At this point, I knew I
needed help.

I asked two students at Saint Mary's College of Minnesota, Mary Beaner and Bernie Buehler, to help in the
selection. Also, I requested that Leiha Bowman invite four
of her Cotter High School students to help; Annessa Piper,
Cassandra Lambrecht, Colm Fitzmaurice, and Jayson
Gerth consented to assist me. This team of students
studied the prayers and helped select the ones that appear
in this book. Their contribution was indispensable and is
greatly appreciated.

Using the Prayers

Teenagers, religious educators, youth ministers, and retreat staff may find the prayers useful in a variety of settings and situations: to start a class, to give focus to a prayer session, and so on. Many of the prayers could also trigger discussions about topics important to teenagers.

Before starting a prayer, you may wish to recall God's presence for your group. Such a reminder calms people and prepares them to attend to the prayer being read. To assist you, three different calls inviting God's presence are listed at the beginning of each part of the book (see pages 11, 28, 40, and 60).

Most of the prayers have final lines that finish them off nicely. However, after reading a prayer, you may wish to invite those praying with you to share insights or petitions related to the prayer. Or you may want to give people a moment to pray silently.

This book of prayers could also be a helpful gift to parents of teenagers. The prayers can remind adults that despite appearances sometimes to the contrary, teenagers have a unique and lively perspective on faith, the world, and themselves. The prayers may open avenues of much-needed teen-parent communication.

A Final Word of Thanks

Great thanks are due to all the students who allowed their prayers and reflections to be submitted for consideration. The only unpleasant aspect of editing this book was having to eliminate so many wonderful prayers. They just could not all go into the book. So, thank you all for your contributions and understanding.

Thanks also go to all the religious educators throughout the United States who sent in the hundreds of prayers received. Your cooperation made the book possible.

I hope all you who pray these prayers find consolation, inspiration, and great hope.

Carl Koch, FSC
Editor

1

Personal Matters

Recalling God's Presence

- Let us remember that God is with us now.
- God, be with us now as we pray.
- Gracious God, we stand in your presence to pray.

Prayers

☆ ☆ ☆ ☆ ☆

Oh, my God, I beg of you, grant me
food in my stomach,
a roof over my head,
a shirt on my back,
a smile on my face,
warmth on my shoulder,
the truth on my tongue,
the light in my eyes,
the love of God and humankind in my heart.
And, God, most of all,
just when I think that the world has turned against me,
then reveal how much
I am truly loved by you and your children.
Through Christ our Savior. Amen.

Chuck
Saint John's High School, Shrewsbury, MA

Loving God,

Please help us all to realize how important we all are in this great big world. Never let each of us forget our individuality as one of your children. When the times get tough and our life seems to be headed in no definite direction, let us realize that if we turn to you we will once again find meaning to our life and a path to follow. Through your divine wisdom and strength we can find meaning in the things that really matter, such as our friends, our parents, and our faith in you. Help us to let you enter into our life. Amen.

Mary Peterson
Eastside Catholic High School, Bellevue, WA

☆ ☆ ☆ ☆ ☆

A Lamentation

Oh, God, do you hear me calling
in the darkest part of night?
I look to you for guidance
but cannot feel your presence.
Oh, help me to overcome this hell
that I am living.

I sit and cry in confusion.
What have I done to deserve this?
Is it what I have done
or what I have not done?
Oh, God, please help me to find
the cure for evil in my world.

Even if I see just a light in the distance,
to know you are there,
I will feel motivation to continue my journey.
Give me the strength to travel my path,
but, God, don't make me walk alone . . .
for I am a heart with loving intentions.

Jennifer Filkins
Gabriel Richard High School, Riverview, MI

☆ ☆ ☆ ☆ ☆

God, you've accomplished many wondrous deeds and blessed us countless times with your gifts, but now I especially thank you for Fridays. My brain is mush, my girlfriend is sick, and next week is beginning to look like a bummer. I really need a vacation to prepare for future events and to collect myself mentally and spiritually. I pray for strength and guidance in all my daily tasks, that I may serve you better day by day. For this and everything else in an otherwise beautiful life, I thank you.

Lumen Christi High School, Jackson, MI

☆ ☆ ☆ ☆ ☆

God, help us to have peace of mind and a sense of moral confidence to know in our heart what is right and wrong. Give us strength to make wise decisions and the courage to stand by our convictions—even in the face of adversity or pressure from our peers. Help us to be happy with ourselves and the path we have taken. And love us when we stray from what is right, so that your love may be our guide. Amen.

Kay Doane
Cardinal Gibbons High School, Raleigh, NC

☆ ☆ ☆ ☆ ☆

Dear God,

My studies in school have been steadily decreasing. I've become awfully lazy and can't seem to do any homework or study for any tests. I don't seem to be able to concentrate as well as I could in the beginning of the year. Why is this? I was wondering if you could possibly give me the strength to overcome this laziness and begin to concentrate again. This would greatly improve my self-confidence and make me know that no matter how boring or hard something may seem, it still can be accomplished.

Mark Kubashigawa
Saint Louis School for Boys, Honolulu, HI

☆ ☆ ☆ ☆ ☆

Dear God,

    When confusion sets in about the purpose of my life, like that which Jesus went through, send me help in the form of patience and wisdom to sort it through.

Mark W.
Holy Cross High School, Marine City, MI

☆ ☆ ☆ ☆ ☆

The Humorous Prayer of a Desperate Student

Now I lay me down to study,
I pray the Lord I won't go nutty.
If I fail to learn this junk,
I hope I don't flunk.

But if I do, don't pity me at all,
just lay my bones in Study Hall.
Tell my teachers I've done my best,
then pile the books upon my chest.

Now I lay me down to rest,
I hope I pass tomorrow's test.
Should I die before I wake,
it's one less test I'll have to take!

John S. Reach, Jr.
Archmere, Claymont, DE

☆ ☆ ☆ ☆ ☆

God—

    Keep me from being sandwiched by two huge semis, being taken hostage by suburban terrorists, getting my head squashed by one of those hospital beds, getting killed by a swarm of killer bees, and getting kidnapped by the same aliens who took the King of Rock and Roll. But, God, most of all, keep me from drifting into the absurd. Amen.

Jerome Nicolas
Saint Anthony High School, Wailuku, Maui, HI

☆ ☆ ☆ ☆ ☆

Tell me, my God, why my life is a street without light. I fight off loneliness and depression. Why, God, must I be burdened with these hardships, in my already hard life?

Must I live and die alone? May I never share with another? What is my destination? What have you planned? Guide me, God, with your loving hand, because your love and kindness are unmatched.

Gabriel Richard High School, Riverview, MI

☆ ☆ ☆ ☆ ☆

Dear God, please help me to keep my life in balance. Let me allow enough time for everything that is important to me. Don't let me neglect the things and persons that should be appreciated most in my life. When I am busy before, during, and after school, let me leave my frustrations and tiredness behind, so that I won't take them out on those closest to me. I make this prayer through Christ our Lord. Amen.

Jerry Vogt
Lumen Christi High School, Jackson, MI

☆ ☆ ☆ ☆ ☆

Jesus, give me the conviction to believe in myself, to love myself, and to give of myself. I have many good qualities, so help me not to envy the qualities of other people or friends. Instead, help me to admire and respect those qualities, as I respect my own.

Jesus, give me the confidence I need to be the best I can be to myself and to others.

Lisa Alef
Bishop Foley High School, Madison Heights, MI

☆ ☆ ☆ ☆ ☆

Dear God,
Let your light shine
down upon my face.
Scatter my sins
across the sun without a trace.
Enlighten the road
that I must follow.
Fill my heart and soul,
sometimes hollow.
Take me to heart again,
once and forever,
and give me strength
to face all endeavors.
You gave me life to love,
so I may love to give life.
Help me through my pain and strife.
Hold me close,
never let me go.
Give me love,
that I might show it to all.

Don Bosco Technical High School, Boston, MA

☆ ☆ ☆ ☆ ☆

Today is here. Help us not to worry about what happened
yesterday or what will happen tomorrow, but to make the
most of today. Help us to live one day at a time and not
to force ourselves to be so caught up in the past or the
future that we cannot enjoy today. Amen.

Cathedral High School, Indianapolis, IN

☆ ☆ ☆ ☆ ☆

God, please help me to deal with people who do not
understand me, and forgive me for the times that I do
not understand others. You understand everything and
everyone.

Randy Mc Nally
Saint Catherine of Bologna School, Ringwood, NJ

☆ ☆ ☆ ☆ ☆

"Anyone who is trustworthy in little things is trustworthy in great. . . ." (Luke 16:10)

In this passage, Luke is saying that either you are always faithful, or you are never to be counted on to be faithful. You can't just say that it is a little thing, and it doesn't matter. Everything counts; nothing is without consequence. The little things build character and strength to follow what you believe.

Teresa Griffin
Notre Dame High School, Batavia, NY

☆ ☆ ☆ ☆ ☆

God, I've noticed that the more I believe in you, the better I become at believing in myself.

Thank you for the things that you have given me. I express my gratitude by not taking for granted what you have given me.

God, please forgive me for the stupid things I do. I'm just fifteen years old, and I don't know everything. So please forgive me. I always try my best to be good. One thing I always try to use is the gifts of life that are there but unused.

God, please help those people who have problems, who are not happy in life, and who are suffering. Help me make a change in people's life, and please help my family and me stay by you. I'll be good today.

Angela
Paramus Catholic Girls Regional High School, Paramus, NJ

☆ ☆ ☆ ☆ ☆

God, grant us the strength we need to overcome the difficulties we face each day. Let our disappointments become opportunities for growth. Through evil, help us seek good, and through you, we may find eternal peace. Amen.

Cathedral High School, Indianapolis, IN

☆ ☆ ☆ ☆ ☆

O God, I think I need your help right now. My patience is
running thin. There always seems to be a problem, whether it is school or family or personal. Just give me a little
strength to pull through. Lack of patience seems to cloud
common sense, as anger slowly rises. So patience, anger,
and common sense run almost hand in hand. All I ask is a
little more of the first, and I'll work on the other two.
Amen.

David Polesky
Archbishop John Carroll High School, Radnor, PA

☆ ☆ ☆ ☆ ☆

God, you have made a ton of average people;
motivation and perseverance
are what will set us apart in the end.
I ask you to help me persevere,
through the troubles that always steer me away from your
    love.
Please help me to overcome the disappointment
when a goal is just too far out of reach,
and help me realize
that defeat is always a two-way street.
Please don't let failure ruin my hope,
because any average person can mope.
But instead, help me rise to new heights and challenges,
being set aside from the individual
who simply "threw in the towel."
I can only do so much,
but in that is a whole world of potential.
I just ask for your guidance and nourishment,
because when it's time for the true test,
no one will be able to put down my best!

Mark Orler
Billings Central Catholic High School, Billings, MT

☆ ☆ ☆ ☆ ☆

God,
You have given light to shine on our world,
but we have turned it into darkness.
    Please help us, God.
You have given us your unconditional love,
but we have turned our back on it.
    Please help us, God.
You have given us your Son,
but few love and follow his teachings.
    Please help us, God.
    Please help us.

Daniel Moller
Saint Frederick High School, Monroe, LA

☆ ☆ ☆ ☆ ☆

So many times, God, I feel as though nothing I do or say
is right; everything turns upside down and I am lost. Help
me, God, to see the light. Guide me. Allow me to follow
your footsteps along the right path. God, send me a sign.
Let me know that I am going in the right direction. Let
me serve you as you have served me.

Ann Pilon
Towson Catholic High School, Towson, MD

☆ ☆ ☆ ☆ ☆

I have locked myself in my own world, God. The door is
locked. There is no key. It is very lonely, God. It is very
dark and very cold. People knock, God. They want to
come in. How can I let them?
    Many times in our life we feel lonely. Often enough
we feel abandoned by others, we feel drowned in our
sorrows and that no one cares or loves us. Our family
loves us. God loves us. For all those times that we have
felt lonely and locked ourselves behind doors, afraid of
letting people in, may we always be able to turn to God,
for it is he who can unlock the door.

Saint Anthony's Parish, El Segundo, CA

☆ ☆ ☆ ☆ ☆

God, help me when my dreams are unclear,
when love seems to be so unfair.
Let me take my dreams in my hand.
Let me know that love will come another day.
But most of all, let me know you are here to stay.

God, and all the saints of heaven,
hear my silent screams.
For it may be that only those in heaven
can see what this broken heart
and shattered dreams cannot.

Guide me from above.
Show the blind what they must see.
Help the dreamers believe.
But most of all, let me know
that you know what is best for me.

Sean Romero
Saint Catherine Indian School, Santa Fe, NM

☆ ☆ ☆ ☆ ☆

God,
Give us strength to do as we feel,
not as others want us to do.
Give us strength to forget, and accept,
in times of misery, defeat, and regret.
Give us strength to overcome our fears,
especially of the unknown,
for we shall be open-minded.
We thank you, God, for loving us,
and we ask you for strength
to overcome all our weaknesses.
Please, be with us forever and ever.
Amen.

Matthew Flynn
Saint John Vianney High School, Holmdel, NJ

☆ ☆ ☆ ☆ ☆

God, remember the time we played together;
you were a rainbow and I slid down your colors.
I danced beneath your brilliant light,
and that night you covered me with your colors,
and I was safe.

Today, however, I feel that you are a dark forest.
Although you surround me, I still feel lost and alone.
God, I'm scared.

I wish we could go back to playing,
but first I want us to be a tree.
You can be the trunk and I the branches.
Together we will stand,
you holding and supporting me.
And I will spread my branches over you,
reaching out with my love.
Together we can never fall.

Kristine Minione
Presentation High School, San Jose, CA

☆ ☆ ☆ ☆ ☆

God, relieve me of my doubts.
Help me believe in myself.
I feel insecure and scared sometimes,
and I need your help when I feel this way.

Give me your guidance to vanish my doubts
about Jesus and my religion.
Don't let me lose my insights in life.
And above all, don't let me lose my faith in you.

Please let me possess open-mindedness and understanding,
so I can use my talents to the fullest,
to learn to trust in the people I doubt the most
and be the best possible person I can.

Janis Elko, Tara-Lea Aleszczyk, Alexandra Pinkal,
Beth Schademann, Kathy Keefe
Bishop George Ahr High School, Edison, NJ

☆ ☆ ☆ ☆ ☆

Dear God, help me to keep my dreams alive, my ideas burning bright. Help me not to give up, no matter how crushed. Help me to have faith in others and faith in you. Help me to work with others to accomplish my dreams, to make their dreams my dreams. Nothing is impossible, as long as I have faith and hope in God and my friends.

Sarah Neppl
Saint Edmond High School, Fort Dodge, IA

☆ ☆ ☆ ☆ ☆

I see no meaning in my life. No importance, barely anything significant. People tell me what to do, I do it, it's over. There must be meaning to everything. Everyone was put on this earth to do something. What about me? Was I forgotten? Help me find it.

Elizabeth Angulo
Mount de Chantal Visitation Academy, Wheeling, WV

☆ ☆ ☆ ☆ ☆

Lately, I haven't had a lot of time for God or prayer. My schedule just seems so filled that I can't find time for personal conversation with God. In the morning, I have to rush to get a decent breakfast before taking my two little brothers to grade school, and then myself and my sister to high school. During my free period, I'm forced to get a start on my homework. After school, I have to get ready for practice, no matter which season we're in. After practice, I shower, eat, and continue to work on my homework. It's almost always late by the time I've finished my homework, so I go straight to bed. If I watch TV or talk on the phone, I go to bed even later. It gets so that I'm always tired, and I feel as if I'm going to spread myself a little too thin one of these days. I look forward to weekends and days off just so I can catch up on a little bit of sleep. Meanwhile, God is getting shoved out of the picture.

Mark Holdener
John F. Kennedy Catholic High School, Manchester, MO

☆ ☆ ☆ ☆ ☆

God, every day as I grow older,
burdens seem to pile up.
As adulthood eases closer and closer,
the pressures about college and choosing a career
become greater and greater.

Help me, God, to deal with these responsibilities,
which affect my future.
Let me turn to you and look for help
when these decisions become too great
to make on my own.

I know I can't expect you
to make a decision for me,
but knowing that you're there
and that you care
really means a lot to me.

Thank you for the past;
be with me in the future.

Amen.

Bob Maciejewski
Bishop Foley High School, Madison Heights, MI

☆ ☆ ☆ ☆ ☆

God! I can't seem to pull myself together anymore. I never
seem to have a moment of peace. There's so much on my
mind. I can't keep up with my problems between my
family, friends, and school anymore. It's just all so compli-
cated and confusing. Each time I finally do resolve one
problem, a million others face me. I even have a hard
time keeping up with you, God. I'm ready to give up.
Please help me believe in myself and you. Thank you for
always believing in me!

Kelly Cox
Thomas More Prep–Marian, Hays, KS

Who Am I?

I am a person like no one else in the world.
I am the people I have met.
I am the experiences I have had.

I am the mistakes I have made
    and the wisdom I have gained from them.
I am the lessons I have learned
    and the ones I have given.
I am the good times in my life
    and the bad ones too.
I am the emotions I have felt
    and the thoughts I have thought.

God, I am the life I have lived.
Although it's not a perfect one,
understand that I'm doing the best I can
with what you have given me.
Because all that I have to work with . . . is me.

Tom Moore
Bishop Foley High School, Madison Heights, MI

Dear God,
    Sometimes I feel no one understands me. I don't understand me. Do you? I'm stuck between childhood and adulthood. I confuse others and myself. When I make decisions, I'm trapped between what I want to do and what I should do. When I'm with my friends, it's hard to be an individual without being an outcast. It's hard not to drink, smoke, and do drugs when everyone around me does. Then I think of you. My problems seem small next to yours. When I feel that I have no strength to do right, I think of all you did for me. Thank you. It helps me keep life in perspective. (But please, don't forget me; I still need your help.)

Missy Naul
Saint Frederick High School, Monroe, LA

☆ ☆ ☆ ☆ ☆

Dear God, help me to make the right decisions while I am growing up. Please don't let my friends push me into things that I don't want to do, such as drugs and alcohol. If I do make a wrong decision, help me to be strong enough to make it right. Lastly, help me become a good, moral person, so I can make good decisions in my life. Amen.

Jamie Formanek
Saint Joseph High School, Westchester, IL

☆ ☆ ☆ ☆ ☆

God, enter our heart and mind.
We are making important decisions;
please help us
to make good ones.

God, you were not popular or athletic.
You did not have a nice car or wardrobe.
Help us look at this example
and realize that the heart and soul make one great!

God, we sometimes put others down
or deny our parents and teachers.
Help us with courage
to love, support, and extend a helping hand.

God, we often make mistakes,
but help us realize that,
through prayer,
all teenagers' souls may be blessed.

Amen.

Terra Ryan
Thomas More Prep–Marian, Hays, KS

☆ ☆ ☆ ☆ ☆

Many times, Jesus, you dared to be different. When you were ridiculed, you did not fight; when you were persecuted, you endured pain; when you were laughed at, you remained quiet.

Jesus, help me not to conform to the standards of others. Give me strength to be original, and keep me from succumbing to the pressures of others. Guide me through the times in which I am tempted to do what is wrong.

Mayra Colon
Lancaster Catholic High School, Lancaster, PA

☆ ☆ ☆ ☆ ☆

God, when I was younger, I used to pray to you daily. Now, as I grow up, I seem to be losing you along with my childhood days and ways. I almost, and at times do, feel guilty to ask for your guidance when I'm in need. There are so many distractions in life that I'm losing control. Please help me to understand the life that you have given me and the purpose it contains. I'm afraid, God, growing up is hard to do! Amen.

Katie Kelly
Archbishop John Carroll High School, Radnor, PA

☆ ☆ ☆ ☆ ☆

God, being a teenager has so many ups and downs, so many vital decisions. It is a time when the pressures of one's peers are at a high, and the choices that are made will inevitably follow people throughout their life. Everyone needs your help, whether they admit it or not. Guide us in your ways so we may live as you would like and make the decisions that will be best for all those concerned. Our whole life is ahead of us, and we put it in your hands.

Michaela Swenson
Billings Central Catholic High School, Billings, MT

☆ ☆ ☆ ☆ ☆

Dear God,
I would like to ask your forgiveness
of my sins,
especially the greatest sin
of taking a life through abortion.
Please don't take this as a confession.
It's more of a prayer.

I also ask that through my mistake,
others will learn not to take intimacy lightly
and that they will respect life.
Please give them the strength and conviction
to do what's right.
Help them realize what true love really is.

Don Bosco Technical High School, Boston, MA

☆ ☆ ☆ ☆ ☆

God, grant me the gift of understanding to really be able
to communicate with those I love and to be able to accept
the unexpected burdens that life sometimes brings. God,
let me continue to believe that everything happens for a
cause and that "good" will always show after "bad."

Lori Bykowski
Bishop George Ahr High School, Edison, NJ

2

Friends and Family

Recalling God's Presence

- God, our friend, you are with us as we pray.
- Holy Friend, you are present among us.
- Be with us, kind God, while we pray.

Prayers

☆ ☆ ☆ ☆ ☆

Thank you, God, for my friend.
She stands at my side through it all—
    the stress   the pain
        the laughter   the joy.
She helps me to see when I am hiding
    behind something that is not me.
She brings me to the realization
    of who I am.
She is my best friend
    my enemy
        my sister in love of God.
I am eternally grateful for knowing her
    and for having her to love.
Thank you, God, for my friend.

Mary Jo Linse
Marian High School, Omaha, NE

☆ ☆ ☆ ☆ ☆

Dear God, we have reached a difficult time in our life. The world we live in is very demanding. We need your help and guidance to find the path we should follow. Please help us to remember the important things in life: family, friendship, prayer, love, and relationships. Never let us get so caught up in material goods that we forget to see the beauty in a sunset and the worth of a smile. Amen.

Maryellen Gruszka
Notre Dame Academy, Worcester, MA

☆ ☆ ☆ ☆ ☆

Today I acknowledge the joy that friends bring into my life. I give thanks to God for the friends with whom I share joy, laughter, companionship, comfort, and understanding. Thanks for my friends who welcome me, who make me feel comfortable in just being me. I think of myself as a friend to all, reaching out and welcoming. I can reach out to others by showing a sincere interest in them. Thank you, God, for making me feel welcome in you. Help me to make others feel welcome too. Amen.

JulieAnn DeSantis
Notre Dame–Bishop Gibbons School, Schenectady, NY

☆ ☆ ☆ ☆ ☆

Why, God, are my parents fighting like this,
when just last week they seemed to be in a state of bliss?
They promised things would never change for me,
while they were giving me sympathy.
But things did change, and that's all right,
because you, God, will be there.
You're always in sight.
Thank you, God, for always being there for me.
Please make me stronger
as my parents' relationship gets weaker.
Amen.

Rob
Archbishop John Carroll High School, Radnor, PA

People that you can trust
are hard to find.

People who care about you
are hard to find.

People who can help you
are hard to find.

People who like you for you
are hard to find.

People just like you
are hard to find.

Mandy White
Pomona Catholic High School, Pomona, CA

Have you ever wondered what it would feel like to be the
last person on earth? Sometimes people feel so alone that
they could refer to themselves and say, "Close enough."
I have been this lonely before, and I realize that there are
others. Even others who feel this way much more fre-
quently than I. Those who walk through the halls of the
school and see everyone else who has someone else they
would rather talk to.

Perhaps we expect that someone else will take the
time, so we don't even bother to smile. What happens if
everyone thinks this same thought? I find myself being
one of those people. "Ah, she looks sad. Her friends will
cheer her up." Now I find myself pondering . . . maybe
those friends do not exist.

I also feel sometimes that my "hello" will not make a
difference anyway, so why bother? But what if my "hello"
lets someone know that they are not the last person on
earth?

Melissa
Billings Central Catholic High School, Billings, MT

☆ ☆ ☆ ☆ ☆

To My Friend

To say we laughed,
to say you taught me,
to say I saw things new,
to say I love you—
none of this is enough,
my friend.

When your world,
with all its ups and downs,
met mine,
with all its ups and downs,
something beautiful
was born.

Tell me it'll never end.
Promise me that wherever I am,
you'll be there too.
Your friendship is precious to me.
I love you,
my dear, dear friend.

Kristine Miller
Immaculate Heart Academy, Washington Township, NJ

☆ ☆ ☆ ☆ ☆

God, last night I had a real talk with my mom. We have
not had a heart-to-heart talk in a long time. Now we
understand each other better and love each other more
deeply. I began to realize how much mothers love their
children and want them to be good and have a happy,
peaceful life. Now I understand that no matter how
difficult it may get, I need to rely on my mom's protec-
tion, love, and caring. I love her for her courage, strong
will, hard work, and honesty. She is a heroine. For her, I
thank you, God.

Chhay Por Taing
Fordham Preparatory School, Bronx, NY

☆ ☆ ☆ ☆ ☆

Dear God,

I've been having a few problems lately concerning my friends who are babies having babies. Each year of high school there has been at least one person I knew who got pregnant. These people who get caught up in this situation are very close to me. This puts pressure on me to either end or continue the friendship. I love my friends dearly and would probably regret not being there at the time they needed me the most, but it seems as if they are being pulled away from me because of their pregnancy.

I would hate to be in the world alone with only you as my friend because I would constantly bother you and want you to be with me at all times. I think that just might be asking for a little too much. I ask you to watch over these people I care deeply about and make them aware that you can be the best friend a person can ever have. Thank you.

Tanya Williams
Buffalo Academy of the Sacred Heart, Buffalo, NY

☆ ☆ ☆ ☆ ☆

Dear God,

I want to thank you for all the people who mean so much to me. My friends, who have helped me through so many ordeals that I thought were the end of the world. My family, who do nothing but worry to see that I am all right. My teachers, who try to guide me the right way. Thank you for all the people who have tried to help. Even though I know the only way to cure my depression is to help myself. And thank you for helping me realize that. But mostly, thank you for being there. I know I don't always make the best decisions, but thank you for trusting me enough to decide. Amen.

Shannon Kavanaugh
Niagara Catholic High School, Niagara Falls, NY

Dear God,

It seems lately that I've been having a hard time making new friends. If you could, please give me the strength and courage to make it through each day with my head up high and without getting depressed and frustrated with myself. I know it takes time to make new friends, but I am very impatient and excited about making new friends. Help and guide me through each day to bring happiness to someone's day.

Gabriel Richard High School, Riverview, MI

So many times, I get so caught up in schoolwork and activities that I forget the most important things in life, which are family and friends. Help me to take time out of my busy life schedule to spend quality time with the people who are most important to me, in order to let them know that they are special and a vital part of my life. Let me always be sensitive to their feelings so that I may be a better friend. Amen.

Kristin Menconi
Marian Catholic High School, Tamaqua, PA

Dear God,

Help my classmates and me to do our best today. Let us never give up or quit. We know we may be tempted to do something wrong, but we promise to try to do what we think is right. Keep us safe during any activities that we may perform today. Help us to settle any disagreements we have with friends. We ask that you will continue to keep our family safe and healthy. Let us be fair in judging others, and let us enjoy life more today. Remember, God, that we will always try to do our best to please you. Amen.

Brian Chmiel
Saint Joseph High School, Westchester, IL

☆ ☆ ☆ ☆ ☆

When my best friend died, a part of my soul died. I stopped eating, quit doing homework and studying, and destroyed most of my friendships. It's not that I was angry at him for leaving, but that I was angry at myself for not saying "good-bye" or how much he meant to me.

As the months passed slowly, I kept the same attitude. I even attempted suicide. Then his mother invited me to their home. After days of hesitation, I agreed. Later we went to his grave. She put her hand on it and said, "He's in there," then, placing her hand on my chest, added, "but he's still in there. And he always will be. And if you close out the world when you pray to him with your heart, you can hear him answer." Then we embraced and cried.

Now, today, exactly a year to his death, I still feel him in my heart and pray to him. And you know, if I'm really concentrating, I can actually hear him answer!

J. C.
Saint Catherine's High School, Racine, WI

☆ ☆ ☆ ☆ ☆

Dear God,

Is it wrong to have idols? Someone to look up to? I know we're supposed to imitate you, not some imperfect human figure. But I have an idol.

No—cancel that . . . I *used* to have an idol. Mine just overdosed on cocaine.

Who can I believe in? Why does it so often seem that someone so fortunate as to become famous makes the mistake of using drugs or abusing alcohol?

Why can't they just find an inner peace and satisfaction with you and the use of their talents?

Please, God, help us to always keep in touch with ourselves so that never happens to me or any of my friends.

Jenny Darrin
Bishop Foley High School, Madison Heights, MI

☆ ☆ ☆ ☆ ☆

For the times I am cruel to my sister,
    I ask your forgiveness.
For the times I take my frustration out on my family,
    I ask your forgiveness.
For the times I treat other people unfairly,
    not giving them a fair chance,
    I ask your forgiveness.
For the times I judge others
    by anything other than what's inside,
    I ask your forgiveness.
For the times I procrastinate
    and don't get my responsibilities accomplished,
    I ask your forgiveness.
For the times I leave other people out
    or make them feel unimportant,
    I ask your forgiveness.
For the times I fail to think of you
    and let my religion take a backseat,
    I ask your forgiveness.
For the times I let fun get in the way of work,
    I ask your forgiveness.
For the times I am selfish,
    I ask your forgiveness.
Amen.

Jennifer Zimmers
Divine Savior Holy Angels High School, Milwaukee, WI

☆ ☆ ☆ ☆ ☆

God, thank you for the gift of my best friend. I realize that she would not be my best friend if I did not give her reason. Help me to be the best friend that I can to her. Allow me to realize that friends are a gift I give to myself and can also be something I can chase away from myself. Help me to respect my best friend and treat her as I would like to be treated.

Michelle Briand
Arlington Catholic High School, Arlington, MA

Dear God,

Sometimes I get caught up in personal wants and yell at those who love me. I don't always see the true good in everybody, and so I make fun of them. Help me to be more patient today with those around me. Let me stop and think of the consequences before I do things that are wrong. Teach me to be more understanding with the people in my life. God, make me an instrument of your peace.

Michael Schoenrock
Bishop Foley High School, Madison Heights, MI

Dear God,

I want to ask your blessing for my parents. Help us to build a strong and happy relationship. I love my parents, but I really don't know how to show my love to them. So, help me God.

Ben Yip
Saint Louis School for Boys, Honolulu, HI

Dear God,

The word *family* means a lot to me, but I think the most important thing it brings to mind is love. That's what a family is made of. If you didn't have love in your family, then it would just be a group of people living in the same house with you.

But love isn't the only thing a family needs. It also needs respect, hope, communication, and mutual agreements. And it needs to have fun together.

God, help me to give the members of my family what they give me, and more. Help me learn to appreciate and love them even more than I do now. Amen.

Kelly Johnson
Bishop Foley High School, Madison Heights, MI

☆ ☆ ☆ ☆ ☆

Dear God,

I don't seem to talk to you that much anymore, not nearly as much as I used to. It's not that I don't care anymore. I do, and I really need your love and your guidance more than ever now.

My life's been kind of hectic for a while, but you knew that. I'm just so confused about everything that's been happening lately. I can't even explain exactly why I'm so confused; I just am. I know it's because there's so much going on in my life that I don't like or don't understand or that frightens me. I often get very depressed and terrified.

Maybe it's because two people very close to me are having serious problems—I mean *serious*. I've never dealt with these problems before—well, I dealt with suicide a while back with another friend, and that was scary enough. It's frightening when you hear someone talk about suicide. I know my friend is getting help, but how do I know she'll hang on? And what can I say to her to ease her pain? And why am I just standing by watching another friend starve herself to death? Is there any way I can help her or comfort her? I'm worried about the future too, what with college just around the corner and some deteriorating relationships.

I know that deep down I love the people close to me, but now, with all this, I'm not sure what I feel anymore. I guess I just want to know that everything will turn out okay, but what if it doesn't? Please, God, help me in whatever way you can, and I'll try to be patient.

Amy Csizmar
Buffalo Academy of the Sacred Heart, Buffalo, NY

☆ ☆ ☆ ☆ ☆

Love—
is necessary
makes me happy
makes me what I am
is what I give
is what I want to give
is why God helps us
is why people help each other
is what keeps us alive
is inside everyone
is what I want
is freely given and received
is selflessness
is terrific.
Love is the "soul food" of my existence.
Salesian High School, Richmond, CA

☆ ☆ ☆ ☆ ☆

You are my friend
    and I am yours.
        Together we've opened
            countless doors.

I know right now
    that you need a hand.
        So don't worry, my friend,
            by you I'll stand.

I will be there with you
    in your time of need.
        You're not alone,
            I'll take the lead.

I know one day
    that I'll need a friend.
        And we'll be together
            to the very end.

Jennifer Cassell
Villa Maria Academy, Buffalo, NY

☆ ☆ ☆ ☆ ☆

Dear God,

As I walk through the halls at school,
I notice the familiar faces
of those I call my friends.

They can put me in a good mood
with a friendly smile
or just a simple "hello."

I'm thankful for my friends, God,
because they make me feel that I'm important;
I feel as if I'm needed
when a friend comes to me with a problem.

Please help me to be a true friend to others
and to give back to them,
through friendship,
what they have given to me.

Karen Rumph
Bishop Foley High School, Madison Heights, MI

☆ ☆ ☆ ☆ ☆

God, for all the people who try to be better and just keep
failing, help them because they start to lose their self-
confidence, and then they don't want to try anymore.
Help all the kids of divorced parents because often they
feel the divorce is their fault. To help relieve their pain,
show them it's not their fault. Amen.

Kevin McIntyre
Saint Joseph High School, Westchester, IL

3

The Big Picture

Recalling God's Presence

- Creator God, be present with us at this time.
- We acknowledge your presence, creator of the universe.
- Let us remember that when we gather in God's name, God is in our midst.

Prayers

☆ ☆ ☆ ☆ ☆

This may sound crazy, but I just went to a great funeral. Sure, it was sad because my friend was grieving over someone she loved dearly, but it made me feel so good to be there for her. Just to hold and hug her in that beautiful church was comforting to us both. Every time I began to feel sad, I just thought how the person who died is going somewhere better and more peaceful.

As I sat in the pew, I thanked God for the life given to us. Life's significance is seen at a funeral when everyone comes together with love and faith to show how much the person who died meant. After shedding a few tears, I left that mass with a refreshed feeling and a lot of hope.

Jennifer Hejaily
Buffalo Academy of the Sacred Heart, Buffalo, NY

☆ ☆ ☆ ☆ ☆

As always, God, I owe you many thanks for many things.
Thank you for good test scores; good weather (no snow,
rain, hail, or ice); enjoyable homework assignments;
certain newly married couples; the gift of music and gigs
that pay; experiments that make sense, don't explode, and
aren't extraordinarily difficult; people who survive
through serious health difficulties; toppling communist
governments and religious freedom for Ukrainians; good
teachers; and all the other blessings that I take for granted
on a daily basis—oh, yes, and for optimism.

Lumen Christi High School, Jackson, MI

☆ ☆ ☆ ☆ ☆

God, with the dawn of a new decade upon us, our world is
in a desperate search for hope. We seek peace in the world
and an end to cruel injustices. We aspire to become the
people of generosity and selflessness we are called to be.
Show us how to be leaders in the struggle for a peaceful
world. Help us to be unafraid of what others will say
about us and to courageously follow the example of your
son, Jesus Christ. Keep alive in our mind and heart the
desire for a better world, and help us to be able to truly
say, "Yes, I can make a difference." Through Jesus Christ,
our Lord. Amen.

Elizabeth Mee
Saint Basil Academy, Philadelphia, PA

☆ ☆ ☆ ☆ ☆

In this world, there are so many different opposing forces.
Stress, war, and hatred seem to be sown, instead of love,
peace, and concern. Help us to see the goodness in others,
and help us to be instigators of peace. Let us love one
another as you have loved us, God, and help us to be the
beginning of a peaceful time.

Suzy McEwan
Notre Dame–Bishop Gibbons School, Schenectady, NY

☆ ☆ ☆ ☆ ☆

Please come to our assistance.
Let justice travel like the wind.
Do not forget us who are poor.
You have seen and felt our distress and grief.
You watch us and take us into your hands.
You listen to the wants of us who are humble,
and you bring strength to our heart.
Every day you renew our life!
We will renew ourselves in you!
Give us, we pray, a greater willingness
to love and care for all people,
and confidence in the action of your grace
in us and throughout your Church.
In your name, we pray.
Amen.

Kelli Schmitt
Nativity Parish, Fargo, ND

☆ ☆ ☆ ☆ ☆

A prayer for the homeless and those less fortunate than we,
when our heart is filled at Christmas
with mistletoe and holly.
A prayer for people whose expectations are too great;
may they understand that no human is perfect
and all may sometimes need a helping hand.
A prayer for those in sorrow or sadness;
may God fill their heart
with joy and happiness.
A prayer for the low in spirit,
whom others sometimes like to attack;
may they not say false things about anyone,
until they know the facts.
This is a prayer made for you and me;
this is a prayer made for everybody.

Kathleen Marie Aguinaga
Saint Barbara High School, Chicago, IL

☆ ☆ ☆ ☆ ☆

I have just finished reading an article in the opinion section of the *Los Angeles Times* on the devastating situation in El Salvador. The very few who try to help the poor, the dying, the sick, and the hungry of El Salvador are jailed, tortured, or murdered.

The government claims that it is not for religious matters that these people are persecuted, but only when these men and women step outside of their religious duties and meddle in the political, social, and economic affairs. The government has the power to murder anyone who stands in its way, no matter how innocent their intentions may be. The government expects the churches to preach the word of God, but not to practice it. The government expects Christians to separate their faith from their daily life and simply ignore the pain and suffering that surrounds their daily life.

What the government simply does not have the heart to understand is that as brothers and sisters of one faith, these men and women cannot help but reach out when they are called upon for help. They cannot shut their eyes and ears to the cries and tears of agony of their fellow brothers and sisters. As Christians and as human beings, they are there to help those in need. Neither intimidation nor persecution can stand in their way.

May God be with those who are there out of the kindness, courage, and love of their heart.

Liliana Ramirez
Saint Augustine Religious Education, Culver City, CA

☆ ☆ ☆ ☆ ☆

Dear God,

Thank you for this wonderful day that you have given us. Let us make the best out of all our opportunities. Strengthen our faith and make us strong. Give us courage to face the world, and let us always be loving and kind to one another. Bless us and be with us throughout this day. Amen.

Saint Thomas High School, Houston, TX

☆ ☆ ☆ ☆ ☆

We believe in God, yes!
But *why*—*what*—is this bad side of life?
This world is so bad sometimes!
Are you for real, God?
We know we must be here for a reason, we must be!
We hear you want us to be open to you—open.
But God, we don't feel you are open and available for us.
We don't see that.
We don't always see your forgiveness.
But we do know you are a forgiving God!
We can see it in the eyes of those around us
when forgiveness passes between us.
Continue to bear with us, God.
Be patient and love us in our growth toward your blessings.

Senior Retreatants
Saint Louis Parish, Fond du Lac, WI

☆ ☆ ☆ ☆ ☆

I really don't know what the world is coming to when so
many are dying in crack houses, living in boxes, and
killing their young. My concern is not only for my future,
but for the future of the human race. I admit, we human
beings have failed you many times, but I plead for your
help now. Only you can give us hope for the future. So
please, God, help me and the multitude of others to be
moral, kind, giving, faithful persons. Give us strength to
pull our world out of the depths of darkness before it is
too late, and give us the light of hope to continue your
good works. Amen.

Nicole Santavicca
Archbishop John Carroll High School, Radnor, PA

☆ ☆ ☆ ☆ ☆

God, help me to realize that it doesn't matter what clothes people wear, how they cut their hair, or what color their skin is. We are all the same in your eyes, and with this awareness your children can move forward as a family. Discrimination deprives people of not only their civil rights but their human dignity. To overcome the evil challenges of our life we must turn to Christ, the good news of Jesus. Everyone deserves the love that you taught us to give to each other. I guess I am petitioning you not to miraculously solve a problem but to allow for an individual understanding of the violation against you and your word that blatant prejudice and discrimination commit.

Nakela Cook
John Carroll High School, Birmingham, AL

☆ ☆ ☆ ☆ ☆

Creator, save this earth,
    for we are hurting our environment.
We are destroying our precious ozone layer,
    which protects us from our sun's ultraviolet rays.
We are murdering our animals, making furs and food.
We are killing ourselves by chopping down our trees.
We are destroying our crops by using insecticides.
We are polluting our waters by dumping garbage and
    chemicals in them.
We are polluting our air by burning our garbage.
Please, God, save our environment,
    for there are naive people who do not see
        what they are doing.
We are committing suicide, bit by bit.

Karissa Rivera
Mary Louis Academy, Jamaica Estates, NY

☆ ☆ ☆ ☆ ☆

God,
   Today and every day, look down on your children.
Give them strength and endurance to survive the trials
that life brings. Help them find a way to improve their
existence. Bless the children of poverty. Hear their cries
for your mercy. Let your presence be of comfort. Protect
them from harm. We ask this in the name of your son,
our Lord, Jesus Christ. Amen.

Kim LeBlanc
Saint Mary's Academy, Milwaukee, WI

☆ ☆ ☆ ☆ ☆

Help me, God, understand why
the nations go to war
and their people cry.

Help me know what is right to do;
who is right for us;
what nation to look up to.

Tell me, God, what is best:
fighting in wars
or laying our arms to rest.

Tell me how we will
keep the world safe
and not have to kill.

Ritch Galvan
Central Catholic High School, Grand Island, NE

☆ ☆ ☆ ☆ ☆

Dear God, please help the lonely people in the world, that
they may be comforted when they need comfort. Let
them be loved when they need love, and let them be
helped when they need help. Amen.

R. W.
Saint Aloysius High School, Vicksburg, MS

☆ ☆ ☆ ☆ ☆

God,
Bless those who need me.
Bless those I need.
Bring peace to us,
into each of our hearts,
and give us the courage
to spread the love you gave us.
Amen.

Megan Landers
Regina High School, Harper Woods, MI

☆ ☆ ☆ ☆ ☆

I know you love everyone, but what I can't understand is
all the hunger and pain you let into the world. I know it's
not your fault that so many children starve and die, but
it's not their fault either. They can't help it if they are born
into a poor family in a place where there isn't enough
good water to grow food, let alone drink. I ask, dear God,
that you help them, or at least help me to help them. I
will do all I can to help them, but I can do so little by
myself. Please walk beside me and guide me down the
right path. I love you. Amen.

Gabriel Richard High School, Riverview, MI

☆ ☆ ☆ ☆ ☆

God,
    You are the almighty, the most high, the center of all
life. You gave life from the smallest cell to the largest
dinosaur. You gave us your Son and your image. For all
these things and all the others, we thank you. God, with
all the things that you give us, I feel bad asking for more,
but it would be so much easier to get your word across if
there were peace in the world. Amen.

Tim McNeil
John F. Kennedy High School, Warren, OH

☆ ☆ ☆ ☆ ☆

The only incident I can think of when I gave of myself without thinking of what I would get in return was about two years ago. A few of my friends and I went to one of our houses and made *so* many sandwiches and carrot sticks and celery and put each combination into a Ziploc bag. We had about fifty or so bags. We all went down to the Port Authority Bus Terminal on Forty-second Street and distributed them to all the homeless "bums" lying on the floor. I don't think we missed one that day. It was enough to see their face as we gave them lunches for absolutely no reason. Some even talked to us. They were very nice and sweet people. Some wouldn't accept the food, but we tried. I gave of myself that day without thinking of myself even once.

Darlene Medina
Saint Michael High School, New York, NY

☆ ☆ ☆ ☆ ☆

Dear God,

There have been many times in history when you have been portrayed as an old man: the white hair, wrinkled face, and feeble-looking body covered with a flowing robe. Yet, you are all-powerful and all-knowing. Sometimes, on earth, we take our elderly people for granted. We think of them as a waste of time and a waste of money. But maybe if we took a few moments to talk to and listen to older people, we could save a lot of time and money. Give us patience, God, to listen and to learn. Give us tolerance when we don't understand. And give us love so that we may care for older people and so that the next generation will already know what it is taking us so long to learn. Amen.

Kim Richardson
Cardinal Gibbons High School, Raleigh, NC

Dear God,
Each day, as I walk throughout the school with my friends,
I observe a few students who are alone.
Unfortunately, these students do not have many friends.
God, give me the strength
to become friends with these people.
Give me the courage
to "dare to be different."
Also, God, give these people the confidence
to open up to others around them.
Perhaps if we become less snobbish,
and they become less frightened,
lasting friendships could result.
Amen.

Jeanette Mulligan
Marian Catholic High School, Tamaqua, PA

Dear God, I find myself existing in a world where some
live in paradise while others starve. All your creations
were endowed with your greatness, yet the casualties of
selfishness leave the world on unsettled terms. I wish to
bring light upon those who dwell in darkness, food for
those whose stomach yearns for it, and hope for those
who feel as though they can't go on. I ask for your help,
my God, in trying to make our world shine in the reflection of your kindness and wisdom. It seems as though so
many people need help and only a few are there to pro-
vide. I ask you to strike new life into your creations so
they may be able to look and see what they really believe
and feel. This way, the world can reflect the image of its
creator. Amen.

Mark Wesley
Saint Joseph High School, Westchester, IL

☆ ☆ ☆ ☆ ☆

Jesus, there were many times throughout your life when you experienced the same emotions I feel now. Often I forget the fact that you were once a young person like each of us. You worried about the problems facing society, even though they may have been different from the ones we face. You loved your family and friends. You laughed when something brought you joy. Many times you felt pity for those who were suffering, and you even cried at Lazarus's tomb. When you were taken away by those who wanted to convict you, all your friends left you, and you were alone. It probably was difficult for you to explain to those around you that you were the son of God, and you felt discouraged.

Dear Jesus, help each of us to remember these things. Help us to understand and to have insight. Each of us is a special sign of God's love. Help us to see that in each one of us, and never let us be afraid to show our emotions, especially the love that we have for you! Thanks for showing us that it is okay to feel the way we do!

Elizabeth
Holy Cross High School, Marine City, MI

☆ ☆ ☆ ☆ ☆

You made the world so beautiful
and the waters so blue.
But time has erased this beauty.
God, tell me what to do.

The air is polluted with smoke,
the streets are filled with dirt.
God, I know you are disappointed.
God, I know you are hurt.

Give me the strength to clean up your world;
this is all I ask of you.
I'll try my best to do your will.
Please tell me what to do!

Maria Muto
Mount Alvernia High School, Pittsburgh, PA

☆ ☆ ☆ ☆ ☆

God,
Let all the homeless know that
you will keep them warm in your heart.
Let all the hungry know that
you will feed them in spirit.
Let all those who suffer the loss of someone know that
you will console them.
Help all who think that you have abandoned them
    know that
you are with them.

Elvia Barrera
Saint Barbara High School, Chicago, IL

☆ ☆ ☆ ☆ ☆

Don't complain about the world;
every happening has its reason.
There's a place for every time
and a purpose for every season.
I bless you with the poor
and the little ones so weak;
may they teach you to help others
and teach you to be meek.
I bless you with drought lands
where nothing will grow;
may you learn to share your food
and love thereby to sow.
I bless you with family, friends,
and elders who pass away;
I keep them safe in heaven,
so you may be with them someday.
I bless you with odd happenings,
whatever they may be;
never despair about yourself,
for you'll always be safe with me.

Stephanie Allen
Hayden High School, Topeka, KS

☆ ☆ ☆ ☆ ☆

For all those who have fallen,
let them stand with your feet.
For all those who have been blinded,
show them the light through your eyes.
Give them the strength to walk through darkness
and soar with open hearts through the journey of life.

Kim Brock
Towson Catholic High School, Towson, MD

☆ ☆ ☆ ☆ ☆

God, we ask for your blessings and wisdom,
    so that we may be stewards of all your creation.
Help us to care for the earth you have created so
        beautifully.
Teach us to appreciate the land,
    the air that we breathe,
    and the food that the earth nourishes us with.

God, help us to realize
    that we are all brothers and sisters,
    that we must care for one another,
    so that no one goes to bed hungry at night
    and we all have a roof over our head,
    a place to call home.
Help us to think of those who may be lonely
    and may need the reassurance that they are loved.

God, help those who have no respect for the earth,
    who have no respect for others,
    and who have no respect for our elders.
Bless them so that they may be better persons.

Thank you, God. Amen.

Halona Teba
Saint Catherine Indian School, Santa Fe, NM

☆ ☆ ☆ ☆ ☆

God, please help those who do not know,
who do not care,
who do not see
what war can do.
One bomb is all it takes,
and the world is gone forever.

Please, God, help them,
help them to make peace,
to see everyone as they see themselves
and their loved ones,
to love as brothers and sisters,
not as strangers and enemies;
help them to forget about
race, color, and creed.

Help us all become
one big family,
and help us make this
a better world.
Please, God, help us come together
as one.

Karmella Roybal
Saint Catherine Indian School, Santa Fe, NM

☆ ☆ ☆ ☆ ☆

God, your name is great and holy.
When your reign gets here,
earth will be just like heaven.
Please give us every day and what is in it.
And forgive us when we don't do what we're supposed to,
so we can also not hold grudges against other kids.
Please keep us from what we know we're not supposed
     to do.
Thank you.

Henry Carson
DeSales Junior-Senior High School, Walla Walla, WA

☆ ☆ ☆ ☆ ☆

Dear God,

We hear you calling, but we do not always answer. We hear you through the crying of the homeless people, yet we tend to ignore even the presence of them. We hear only our meaningless and senseless problems, although others are much less fortunate. We need to reach out and listen to others when they are in need of our help. God, help us to acknowledge the presence of others in need. Amen.

Kristy Clymer, Esther Sandoval, Maura McHugh
Divine Savior Holy Angels High School, Milwaukee, WI

☆ ☆ ☆ ☆ ☆

Dear God,

You created the world, and we are young adults who will soon have it in our hands. Help us now to make a difference so that we will create new life instead of destroying it. Also help us to use wise judgment in forming opinions about what is right and wrong. Stand by our side, for we are afraid to walk alone. Just be there to listen, and we will answer your call. Through the virgin Mary, mother of God. Amen.

Jennie Lonero
Queen of Peace High School, Burbank, IL

☆ ☆ ☆ ☆ ☆

God, it is easy to ask you for forgiveness, or happiness, or an easy life—and I often do this. But it is much harder to ask for the abilities to forgive, to make others happy when they are down, or to give of myself. Please help me realize that to be forgiven, I need only to forgive; that by giving, I will also receive; and that making life easier for others will enrich my own life as well.

Kathie Delaney
Bishop Foley High School, Madison Heights, MI

☆ ☆ ☆ ☆ ☆

I have been acquainted with this one person several times, but I have never engaged myself in a conversation with her. I work the night shift at K mart, and she comes in regularly to buy only the clothes on clearance. Never have I seen this lady, in her mid-forties, purchase something that cost more than three dollars. Even the very cheap or clearance clothes she tries to get more cheaply by pointing out a hole or stain to me. Every nickel is a major concern of hers. She looks very weary when she counts out her money, penny by penny. It looks as if her hardships have aged her at five times the rate of other people. It looks as if she could eat much more than is available to her because she is very skinny.

At first, without looking, I was bothered by this lady because she would always call me away from my work to the service desk just to squabble over fifty cents. However, once I noticed this woman, she drew me into her circle of suffering. How lucky I am not to fight for a discount of fifty cents just so I can eat breakfast in the morning.

Seeing all this makes me feel guilty for some of my own luxuries that I take for granted. Because of the world's (including my own) self-centeredness, someone is paying the price. Here the case is not obvious because I myself did not make this woman poor, or want her to be poor. However, I am still responsible, as are many others, because I think that if you are not part of the solution then you are part of the problem. We must all do our part to contribute what is possible, not only money but whatever resources and time we can offer.

Maggie Kronk
Mercy High School, Farmington Hills, MI

☆ ☆ ☆ ☆ ☆

God,

Thank you for your love and everything you do for us. Please help those who have been hurt to heal, those who have sinned to be forgiven, those who sometimes do without to be provided for, and those who serve to be acknowledged. Help us to know and understand you better and serve you to the best of our abilities. Amen.

Saint Thomas High School, Houston, TX

☆ ☆ ☆ ☆ ☆

God, too often we label people. We look at the way someone dresses or wears their hair, without taking the time to get to know anything about the real person. All we see is the outside shell. We make fun of people, and sometimes fights even start. Why? Just because they're different from us? Everybody's different in their own way, but some people just show it more than others.

God, help us to realize that people's differences are something to enjoy, not criticize. What a boring world it would be if everybody were exactly the same.

Dave Gorczany
Bishop Foley High School, Madison Heights, MI

☆ ☆ ☆ ☆ ☆

Dear God, please help the people in the world to reconcile their differences. Allow us to help our brothers and sisters everywhere who are in need. Help us to tear down political and social walls that prevent our love from shining through. Let us be the sun for all life. Help us to recognize the good in each one of us and to remove the veil of racism and criticism through which we often view our relationships. Amen.

Sue Walsh
East Catholic High School, Manchester, CT

☆ ☆ ☆ ☆ ☆

An unborn baby . . .
    a human.
To let live or to kill?
It's your choice.

A small heartbeat,
    so hard to hear.
To let go on or to stop?
It's your choice.

A tiny form,
    so delicate and frail.
To let grow or to break?
It's your choice.

A little kick,
    too small to be painful.
To feel or to inflict?
It's your choice.

A feeling,
    so new to you.
To keep or to lose?
It's your choice.

There's something growing in you,
    you can see.
To kill or let be?
It's your choice.

An unborn baby,
    that was you.
To let live!
It was God's choice.

Amy Weber
Villa Maria Academy, Buffalo, NY

☆ ☆ ☆ ☆ ☆

What bothers me is that not enough people feel pain when they see pictures of death camps, hear stories of torture and unjust imprisonment and government in other countries—or even in their own—or watch their environment crumble to dust right before their very eyes. My God, how many people experience pain when (and if) they imagine Christ's death on the cross? This is the pain of separation, of indifference—of hell.

Years ago I made a commitment to make a difference in the world I live in. The roots of this commitment lie in the realization that our lives—the lives of all the beings, plant or animal, that are, were, or ever will be—are ever so tightly intertwined. Every single thing I do affects everyone and everything else: how I spend my money, the profession I choose, the words I speak, the actions I take— or the words I do not speak, the actions I do not take. When I allow myself to become immune to the media, when I choose not to make myself aware of world situations, when I choose to remain silent and inactive, I choose to let the wall remain standing. I choose the pain of hell: separation from God, from life, and from my own self.

The choice to love is the choice to see and recognize the oneness and wholeness of everything. The goal is to knock the wall down and to try to stop the pain of separation and indifference—the pain of hell. The only pain to feel is the pain of conscience, the pain of the unfulfilled needs of so many others, and the pain of love.

Olga Berwid
Saint Francis Preparatory School, Fresh Meadows, NY

Dear God,
When I see the pain and suffering surrounding me,
I feel trapped,
wanting nothing more than to escape.

Please God,
Give me the strength, every day of my life,
to face my troubles up front
and to help others when they are in need of it.

May you stay with me every day of my life, God.

Liliana Ramirez
Saint Augustine Religious Education, Culver City, CA

God, help me to choose the right career. Not the career
that is the most prestigious or makes the most money but
the one that makes me happy. After all, Jesus did not care
about being rich and highly respected, he just wanted to
help people. Please help me pick the career that will best
serve you and other people, because that is the key to
ultimate happiness.

Dave Kotwicki
Bishop Foley High School, Madison Heights, MI

4

Addressing God

Recalling God's Presence

- The God who empowers dwells within us.
- Let us remember that the God of the universe lives among us.
- A kind and merciful God is in our midst, as we pray.

Prayers

☆ ☆ ☆ ☆ ☆

My first experience with God occurred this past summer. One day my sister's boyfriend caught a virus and passed away. He was only nineteen years old and full of life. The day after he died, I went to his wake. I was standing there just looking at him. I had been to many wakes before, but nothing like this one. Even though he was lying there motionless, he looked so alive. Then this strange and unusual feeling came over me, as if nothing were wrong. I felt as if God were in the room, standing next to me. I thought I was crazy, but then it was time to go to church for the funeral. At the cemetery I had that same feeling. I knew then that my sister's boyfriend was okay and that he was in God's care now.

Rosalie
Paramus Catholic Girls Regional High School, Paramus, NJ

Each day as the sun rises and sets,
we all take for granted that it is you
who makes these things happen.

Too often, we become consumed
by what we don't have
and what we cannot control.

We don't realize that
your all-knowing hands can lead us
toward the right path each day.

Once we have reached our destination,
your light will break through,
to make our blind eyes see.

Amen.

Michael McGowan
Pope John Paul II Regional High School, Boca Raton, FL

☆ ☆ ☆ ☆ ☆

You have guided me and have given me strength;
you have made me from dust and have brought me into
     this world;
you have given me parents who love me and friends who
     will always stand by me;
for all this, God—I thank you.
You have shown me the right path to heaven and have
     taught me to serve you and your people;
because of you, my dreams and goals are possible;
for all this, God—I thank you.
You have given me your everlasting love and support;
you have given me your "shoulder" to lean on and your
     faith to believe in;
for all this, God—I thank you.
But most of all, God, you have given me you;
for this, God—I love you. Amen

Katie DeLaveaga
Saint Anthony High School, Wailuku, Maui, HI

☆ ☆ ☆ ☆ ☆

Please understand, God, that when I question my faith, I am growing, not doubting. Life is so confusing. Everything is based on a materialistic level, so to grasp your being, I question the possibility of your existence. In these times, I'm showing fear, not spitefulness. Teens are not rebelling, they're turning toward freedom. Dear God, please understand and help me to take the path of right when all goes wrong. In my developing stages, I ask for patience and guidance through the pathway of life. Amen.

Amy Lipson
Lancaster Catholic High School, Lancaster, PA

☆ ☆ ☆ ☆ ☆

Dear God, help us come closer to you.
It is hard to believe what is unseen,
though your presence is felt internally.
Swim into our mind,
step into our soul.
We live and thrive
because our beating heart is made of your love.
Help us to become closer to you.
God, guide us through your eyes to the Truth.

Keisa Johnson
Saint Bernard High School, Playa Del Rey, CA

☆ ☆ ☆ ☆ ☆

Thank you, God, for the life you have given us. Thank you for the tomorrows, during which we can fix the mistakes we may have made today. Thank you for our family and your love, which bring happiness into the life you have given us. Thank you for the sorrows, which challenge us, and also for soothing our pains. Thank you for your love, which shows us that we can make it through anything as long as we believe in you.

Jennifer Bergin
Notre Dame Academy, Worcester, MA

☆ ☆ ☆ ☆ ☆

God, when I cry out to you, you hear me.
Whenever I'm in trouble, you help me.
Every day I pray to you, but sometimes I can't find comfort.

You, O God, keep me awake and alive.
I think of all the days, months, and years gone by.
I think about you every night.

I ask myself questions about you:
Has God stopped loving me?
Or has God's anger taken the place of compassion?

But what seems to hurt the most
is that most people don't trust and love as they used to.
But I will always remember God's helpfulness.

(Paraphrased from Psalm 77)

Amie Bensman
Saint John High School, Delphos, OH

☆ ☆ ☆ ☆ ☆

Jesus,
When I walk alone,
　　I talk to myself,
　　　knowing that you are listening to me.
I talk to you,
　　telling you my problems.
I tell you about my day
　　and what it was like.
I ask you if you are listening.
There is no answer.
I talk some more,
　　telling you more,
　　but still there is no answer from you.
Then when I feel free
　　from all my problems and thoughts,
　　I know that you, Jesus, were there for me.

Leontine Earl
Saint Catherine Indian School, Santa Fe, NM

☆ ☆ ☆ ☆ ☆

Dear God, with all the problems in my life, the main problem is my being handicapped. I know that you made me this way because you thought that it would be the best thing for me. When I'm all alone at night, sitting in my room just thinking about everything, I think about being like everyone else and how great it would be to be able to walk right. But I do thank you for letting me live today in this horrible world of ours. I thank you for being with my parents and giving them the strength to be able to handle me when I was little. Dear God, thank you for being with me as I go through life.

H. M.
Saint Aloysius High School, Vicksburg, MS

☆ ☆ ☆ ☆ ☆

Dear God,
    Sometimes I wonder, "Where are you? Why aren't you here with me?" Sometimes I forget that you are always there—helping me through, extending your hand, waiting for me to take it.
    Other times I don't want you around. I don't want to listen to you. I let my pride get in the way.
    Please help me to establish a balance between the two, so I can love and follow you more closely.

Bridget Habesland
John S. Burke Catholic High School, Goshen, NY

☆ ☆ ☆ ☆ ☆

God, you are the mighty creator of our life. Everything we have, you've created so perfectly. Every little detail, from our fingerprints to the tiniest cell, you've made with your hands. You are well-known yet mysterious; you have so much power in your hands. You have the power to build and the power to destroy. God, you show nothing but love and compassion toward us.

Jody Kuelbs
Saint Mary's High School, Sleepy Eye, MN

☆ ☆ ☆ ☆ ☆

Sometimes I wonder who I am
and what it means to be me.
I look in the mirror
and see my reflection,
but all I get is another question.
"Who am I?"
"Who made me?"
"Who created this world of ours?"

As I look up into the sky,
looking for the answers to my thoughts,
a powerful sensation hits my face
and fills me with warmth and compassion.
At first I say
it's just the sun,
but then I realize
it's the answers to my questions.

The one who created the sun and the sky
and filled my heart with love and compassion
is the same one who let me be
and placed me in this world.
God is the answer to all my questions
and fills my mind with thoughts.
God is truly the light of the world,
the light that fills my heart.

Michael Kassouf
John Carroll High School, Birmingham, AL

☆ ☆ ☆ ☆ ☆

Boredom! Time is passing, and there's nothing to do. As I
sit here not really concentrating, my mind drifts to
thoughts of you, God. I marvel at your gift of time. How
mysterious it is; how much I take it for granted; how
often I waste it. Thank you for all the time I have, and
show me how to use it well. Amen.

Janet Bockey
Saint John High School, Delphos, OH

☆ ☆ ☆ ☆ ☆

I'm writing because I found the answers to my most
perplexing questions in life. I'm writing because I found
God in myself—I found God in the simplest word I know:
love. It suddenly dawned on me that all creation was
created for a purpose, and all was created out of love. And
the human soul—the essence of life—is 100 percent love.
And God is love. So, God is present in all of us.

Love is what keeps us together, what binds us, what
challenges us. It can't be held or captured—it's as free as
the air! And yet it is full and overflowing, but it doesn't
strangle us, doesn't kill us. To say "I love" is to say "God is
here with me." Every time someone professes love it is a
testimony to the existence of God!

I used to believe that to feel the presence of God you
had to be meditating. But I've found that in just simply
being alive—acknowledging your soul—God is *actively*
present. Here, now, inside of me! And it's no cause to feel
alarm. It's the warmest, deepest, most secure feeling I have
ever known. Because, for once, it feels *real*, and *alive*. I feel
loved from *within* myself. For the first time in a long
time—love comes from within. It binds me, it overflows,
and it's free.

And now I understand why one must love oneself
before one can truly love another. It's simply overwhelm-
ing. No lights, no spectacular drama. Just simply "being."
I understand now that God was always within me. I just
needed to learn how to look at God.

Adelaide Juguilon
Magnificat High School, Rocky River, OH

☆ ☆ ☆ ☆ ☆

Are we at all sure that God wants to hear our prayers? It seems that God has a terrible job. The way most people pray, God must feel like the complaint department in a store. The Almighty must get truly sick of it.

As a result, I no longer really pray to God; I hold conversations with God. Praying is too solemn; I'm sure the Creator prefers being treated as a friend.

God must feel better taking part in a conversation. Perhaps we take God too seriously. God deserves better than the reverence and dread shown to a superior. We ought to treat God as we treat our friends—as someone we can trust and someone we can talk to, someone special!

Jason Bujnosek
Saint Michael's High School, Santa Fe, NM

☆ ☆ ☆ ☆ ☆

Dear Nameless Friend,

I have my questions about God. My faith is diminishing, my church days are numbered, but I know it gets better. Philosophy is no substitute for religion. I don't know where faith lies, but I know how to achieve it. You can achieve it within yourself. If you can't believe in God at this point, believe in you—at least there's something. God will come to you—the Creator is already there. You just have to reach down, find God, and recognize God. Don't worry—it takes time. You sound like you are just in the early stages. Good luck in your soul search.

Hang in there.

Chris Reilly
Saint Rose High School, Belmar, NJ

68

☆ ☆ ☆ ☆ ☆

God,

    I know that you're all around, and you see every-
thing. But then again, where are you when I need you?
Sometimes you are there, but what about those times
when I was really hurt and no one was there to comfort
me? When I feel your presence, I feel that I am invisible
and no one can harm me, but I guess it's just the opposite
when I don't feel your presence. Help me realize that no
matter what I say or do to turn myself against you, I can
always count on you. Amen.

Cyndi Padilla
Pomona Catholic High School, Pomona, CA

☆ ☆ ☆ ☆ ☆

I can count on you
when all around me think
gossiping is fun.
You help me to be silent
and not mean to anyone.

I can count on you
when partying means
having a drink or two.
You help me to refuse
and do what I should do.

I can count on you
when others try to lead me
to do wrong.
You show me how to just say no.
You keep me firm and strong.

And I want you to know
that I'll always try to be
what you want me to be.
Because I can always count on you.
You can always count on me.

Lisa Solis
Stella Maris High School, Rockaway Park, NY

To God

As I see
the flowers blooming in the spring,
    I *see* life.

When I hear
a child screaming for attention,
    I *hear* life.

When I eat
at the dinner table with my family,
    I *taste* life.

When I walk
through a grassy field of flowers,
    I *smell* life.

As I shake hands
with my daily companions,
    I *touch* life.

What I see, hear, taste, smell, and touch
is you, God.
    Thank you!

Bianca DeHoyos
Providence High School, San Antonio, TX

Dear God,
Thank you for everything,
from the sunrise in the morning
to the full moon at night.
Thank you also for the many gifts
you have given us.
From day to day,
I thank you and praise you.

Ira Atencio
Saint Catherine Indian School, Santa Fe, NM

☆ ☆ ☆ ☆ ☆

God as Mother

O Mother, O Creator,
    lend me your hands
    so that I may make America
    a better land.

O Mother, O Weaver,
    lend me your thread
    so that I may knit together for the homeless
    a warm bed.

O Mother, O Baker,
    lend me your yeast
    so that I may make a fine bread
    to put hunger to peace.

O Mother, O Washer,
    lend me your soap
    so that I may cleanse others of troubles
    and help them to cope.

O Mother, O Compassion,
    lend me your heart
    so that I may comfort those
    who have drifted apart.

O Mother, O Wisdom,
    lend me your mind
    so that I may use it to understand others
    and always be kind.

Tina Filiato
Mary Louis Academy, Jamaica Estates, NY

☆ ☆ ☆ ☆ ☆

God, isn't it funny,
    the times we choose to speak;
it's usually when *I'm* down
    or having trouble going to sleep.

I know that you try to speak to me
    every night and every day,
but I usually don't choose to answer
    unless *I* have something to say.

This time I ask no favors,
    no miracle *A*'s on tests,
but, instead, I'd like to thank you
    for the things that I love best.

First, I'd like to thank you for my family,
    as strange as it seems sometimes,
and especially for those little rodents,
    yes, those three darling brothers of mine.

Next, I'd like to thank you for my friends,
    who strengthen me every day
and who, when I'm hurt or in trouble,
    show me a brighter day.

I'd like to thank you for nature,
    the most beautiful gift of all,
from the sweet smell of flowers in spring
    to the awesome colors of fall.

Now, I'd like to thank you
    for being such a wonderful friend
and for all those times you took my broken heart
    and put it back together again.

The last thing that I'm thankful for
    is really a dream come true,
it's something I cherish dearly,
    it's the friendship I have with you.

Tony Grewing
Sacred Heart High School, Muenster, TX

☆ ☆ ☆ ☆ ☆

God Is Everything *but* a Great Big Bore!

I can't really define
someone this rare;
I don't deserve
God's maximum care.
God knows my faults
are worth the blame,
but keeps on loving me
just the same.
God really understands,
and knows my demands.
Lots of my friends
think every day, more and more,
that God is just
a great big bore.
I hope one day
they'll see things my way:
Everything comes and goes,
but God's love will always stay.

Debbie Tran
Madonna High School, Chicago, IL

☆ ☆ ☆ ☆ ☆

God,

Every now and again, we lose sight of what truly is important. We've lost the happy simplicity we had when we were children. We despair in times when there seems to be no relief. Your promises are forgotten in the rush of day-to-day survival.

Sometimes, we need to be reminded that you are always there for us. Even in the bleakest of times, you never once abandoned us. Help us to remember that if our faith remains true, there is nothing in this world that can overcome us. Amen.

Cathy Belleville
Edgewood High School, Madison, WI

☆ ☆ ☆ ☆ ☆

One day I was with the family in the car coming back from somewhere. I don't remember where we went, but it must have been last year because I was reading a chemistry assignment about atoms. I remember suddenly realizing that those tiny little structures were in everything, and that anything around me was made up of millions of them.

I looked out the car window and watched as thousands of trees went by my window every second and stretched all the way to the horizon. (We must have been driving through the mountains in some vast open state.) I watched one tree go by and tried to concentrate on one leaf, trying to imagine that it contained countless little things in it. I realized that God had created every single atom in that leaf—an incredible, unbelievable feat in itself. And then I looked around at the whole forest around it, and I realized that God created all that, too—God created every atom; and then I realized how huge the state was compared with the forest—God created every atom; and I saw how huge the whole world was compared with that state—God created every atom; and I saw how vast the rest of the universe was compared with that single leaf—and God created everything.

I suddenly felt God's power and care. Everything that God made must have been important enough that it was put together out of so many complex pieces. It helped me to realize how petty the little everyday problems were, the problems that we allow to weigh us down and distract us from the amazing beauty all around us.

If I had to choose a symbol for this God experience, I'd choose a leaf.

Charles Becker
Christian Brothers Academy, Lincroft, NJ

☆ ☆ ☆ ☆ ☆

God, I saw a sunset the other night. It made me stop everything I was doing to look. The sunset was just what I needed at the time. It calmed my nerves, made me relax, and helped me basically settle down and get away from the stress I was feeling. I am convinced that the sunset in all its glory was sent by you to help calm me. People say that you work in mysterious ways, and now I understand what they mean. You are everywhere, forever revealing yourself to us. All that you ask of us is to open our eyes and take in your beauty.

Todd Cormier
Billings Central Catholic High School, Billings, MT

☆ ☆ ☆ ☆ ☆

Every now and then, I stop and close my eyes,
and I think of you, God.
There are times life is so wonderful, I can't contain it;
my life is created for your word.
I often praise your glorious grace.
If ever I am sad, I pray for a plan,
and you are always prepared to rescue me.
You know my needs, my joys, and my pain—
you can always tell what is going on.
You will meet every cry of my heart.
You will always offer me a path to you,
and that path is a desire to be with you.
So, I thank you, God, for being my guiding light
that will never burn out.

Dawn Davis
Saint Francis High School, Sacramento, CA

Although I may not always show it,
I am grateful—
grateful for all you have given me:
my family, my health, my friends . . .
everything!

Sometimes I forget how grateful I am
or how grateful I should be.
Sometimes I put that behind me
and move on to better, more glorious things.
You know how I am.

You know I strive to do better,
but don't you know, I do it all for you.
But of course you do.

Suzanne McDonald
Sacred Heart High School, Kingston, MA

☆ ☆ ☆ ☆ ☆

God,
We ask of you guidance and a little more:
guidance in relationships,
guidance in decisions,
guidance in love,
and guidance in worshiping you.

To love just as Jesus,
to decide just as Jesus,
to relate just as Jesus
is our goal.

We thank you, God, for all your blessings—
for everyday blessings,
for the people we love,
for the sun to shine
and the ground to walk on.

Peter Murray
Fordham Preparatory School, Bronx, NY

☆ ☆ ☆ ☆ ☆

Listen

Huh?
What?
I can't hear you; speak louder.
I don't understand what you're saying.

Dear God, I want to do what you want of me,
but I don't know what it is.
You speak to me through people,
but my ears are distracted.
Your presence surrounds me,
but fear and disbelief separate us.
Every day you try so hard,
but my effort is not there.

Teach me, God,
to listen and to hear,
to look and to see,
and to understand and to know.
For the only way to find happiness
is to find you.

Yvette Heide
Bishop Foley High School, Madison Heights, MI

☆ ☆ ☆ ☆ ☆

An experience I had with God occurred while I was jog-
ging with my dog on the sandy shoreline early one summer morning at Seaside Beach. My dog had stopped to
sniff out some seaweed and refused to leave it alone.
While I was waiting for him, I was struck by the stillness
and beauty of the ocean that surrounded me. It caused me
to think of the greatness of God, and how much God
cares for everyone to have created such a beautiful world
for all of us to enjoy. My symbol for my God experience
would be the ocean.

Lynn Pompili
Saint Mary of the Valley High School, Beaverton, OR

☆ ☆ ☆ ☆ ☆

God, you know there are too many bizarre things going on in my life. I don't know what to do. What bother me the most, though, are all the doubts I suddenly have. You know I'm not talking about what I should do about my new zit, or about the gorgeous guy down the street. I'm saying that I've lost you right now. I have all these horrible doubts about religion, God. I mean my Catholicism. I have a really hard time embracing all the values the church dictates. I see how we have made some very bigoted and hypocritical laws and assumptions in the church. I have never doubted you, God. I really believe Jesus is "alive" in the Eucharist, but I don't know about all the taboos and traditions.

Help me, God. Help me pray, and help me believe. Not with the clichés, God; not with what any priest would tell me. That doesn't help. Let me know I can have a personal relationship with you.

Serina Lucero
Saint Michael's High School, Santa Fe, NM

☆ ☆ ☆ ☆ ☆

Dear God,
I can see the beautiful things in this world.
I can hear the drumming of the rain and feel the gentle
     breezes.
But, God, make me more sensitive to the beauty.
Let me see the extraordinary in the ordinary.
Grant that my eyes may see the colors, whether vibrant or
     faint, more clearly for what they are.
May my ears listen to your symphony of sounds more
     intently and the slightest sensations fill every part
     of me.
May the fragile scent of the rose smell sweeter each time
     it's encountered and the magnificent details of the
     earth not be overlooked.

Sheri Harrison
Bishop Foley High School, Madison Heights, MI

☆ ☆ ☆ ☆ ☆

Oh, God, thank you for
    the sun that rises and sets,
    the moon that glows,
    the stars that shine,
    the birds that fly,
    the creatures that run,
    the people that care,
    and the babies that cry.
Oh, God, please bless
    the ocean in which we swim,
    the mountains on which we climb,
    and the homes in which we live.
Oh, God, please watch over
    all children, big and small,
    the life that is growing, the life that is gone,
    and everyone all around.
And please, God,
    guide us through the days that come,
    help us to be there for those in need,
    help us to be loving and understanding,
    and, most importantly, help us always to have faith in
        what we believe.

Heather M. Jones
Santa Margarita High School, Rancho Santa Margarita, CA

☆ ☆ ☆ ☆ ☆

Dear God,
Hope
    is what you give us.
Understanding
    is what you teach us.
Trust
    is what we learn from you.
Friendship
    is what we find in you.
Amen.

Stacy Sherbon
Pope John Paul II Regional High School, Boca Raton, FL

☆ ☆ ☆ ☆ ☆

Dear God,

I want to thank you, most of all for being a good listener.
Even when I don't ask you to hear my words, you are
    always there, and you pay attention anyways.
No matter how much I have to say or how long I chatter
    on, you are always very patient, you never interrupt
    or contradict me, and I know that I can trust you
    with my biggest secrets.
Thank you for listening to me cry for days and days when
    my first "love" didn't work out, and thank you for
    being patient when I prayed for a million different
    things for my birthday.
Thank you for not telling Mom and Dad all the awful
    things that I say about them when I get angry, and
    also thank you for just being silent and giving me the
    opportunity to let my feelings out.
You are never judgmental about anything I say, and I
    don't need to hide anything from you.
You speak no words, yet I know you listen, not just with
    your mind, but with your heart.
Without fail, you are always there when I need you.
When I call, I never get the answering machine or the
    busy signal, any time of night.
You're never too tired to take the time to hear me speak.
Thank you, God, for your attentive ear and for always
    finding my words important enough to listen to.

Motrya Tomycz
Luke M. Powers Catholic High School, Flint, MI

☆ ☆ ☆ ☆ ☆

A great eagle in domination,
    or a lonely sparrow on its own.
A rose in the garden,
    or a simple daisy in the fields.
A vast ocean,
    or a gentle flowing stream.
This is all I dream
    my God to be.

Virginia C. Rishkofski
Villa Maria Academy, Buffalo, NY

☆ ☆ ☆ ☆ ☆

Why do you stand aloof, O God?
Why do you hide yourself in times of trouble?
(Psalm 10:1)

How long, O God? Will you forget me forever? . . .
How long must I bear pain in my soul?
. . . .
Consider and answer me, O God:
give light to my eyes, lest I sleep in death.
(Psalm 13:1–3)

The lines of these two psalms say a lot to me because there have been times when I felt so far away from God, and I couldn't reach God. God wouldn't let me. It was as if God was heading away from me to let me solve the problems, and I didn't know how then.

Now that I am older, I do understand that God wasn't hiding away from me. God was suffering just as much as I was. God was giving me the chance of making my own choices. Now I know that the Almighty never hides from me and will never let me die from sorrow. Jesus is trying to say to me to trust myself as well as to trust him.

Jeannie Campis
Saint Pius V High School, Bronx, NY

☆ ☆ ☆ ☆ ☆

My God,
When pressures from the world around begin to
    trouble me,
my God is always there for me.

When my faith in myself fails,
my God is always there for me.

Thank you, God, for the love that you give me,
it shows in those around me;
my God is always there for me.

My God's words are forever with me,
this is how I know:
my God is always there for me.

Chris Eckenrode
Lancaster Catholic High School, Lancaster, PA

☆ ☆ ☆ ☆ ☆

God, your role in my life
has changed over the years.

When I was young,
my parents took me to church
and taught me about you.
I didn't have a choice
but to follow them.

Now that I am older,
I make my own decisions
about religion.
So, God,
help me make the right decisions about you.

Salesian High School, Richmond, CA

☆ ☆ ☆ ☆ ☆

Remember me
when you see sunshine in the clear blue sky,
when morning glories bloom in the summer,
when you see soft rains in the spring or trickles of
    snowflakes in the winter.
Remember me
as a star guiding you through the night
or as wind breezing through the air.
Remember me
when you hear children laughing, people singing, or
    babies crying.
Remember me
when you're helping out your neighbors by lending an ear
    to listen or a hand to get them back on their feet,
or when you bring a smile to someone's face.
Remember me
when you're loved by your family,
when communion is served,
or when you meditate in prayer.
Never stop to remember me
when you feel down and out;
I'm always here when you need me because I am the
    Savior who died for you,
but I am also your friend and want to help you.
And this is the Remembrance of Me.

Deridré Daniels
John S. Burke Catholic High School, Goshen, NY

Index ☆ ☆ ☆ ☆ ☆ ☆ ☆ ☆ ☆ ☆

DeSales Junior-Senior
High School
Walla Walla, WA
Henry Carson 53

Divine Savior Holy Angels
High School
Milwaukee, WI
Jennifer Zimmers 35
Kristy Clymer 54
Esther Sandoval 54
Maura McHugh 54

Don Bosco Technical
High School
Boston, MA
Anonymous 16
Anonymous 27

East Catholic High School
Manchester, CT
Sue Walsh 56

Eastside Catholic
High School
Bellevue, WA
Mary Peterson 12

Edgewood High School
Madison, WI
Cathy Belleville 72

Fordham Preparatory School
Bronx, NY
Chhay Por Taing 31
Peter Murray 75

Gabriel Richard High School
Riverview, MI
Jennifer Filkins 12
Anonymous 15
Anonymous 33
Anonymous 47

Hayden High School
Topeka, KS
Stephanie Allen 51

Holy Cross High School
Marine City, MI
Mark W. 14
Elizabeth 50

Immaculate Heart Academy
Washington Township, NJ
Kristine Miller 31

John Carroll High School
Birmingham, AL
Nakela Cook 45
Michael Kassouf 65

John F. Kennedy Catholic
High School
Manchester, MO
Mark Holdener 22

John F. Kennedy
High School
Warren, OH
Tim McNeil 47

John S. Burke Catholic
High School
Goshen, NY
Bridget Habesland 64
Deridré Daniels 82

Lancaster Catholic
High School
Lancaster, PA
Mayra Colon 26
Amy Lipson 62
Chris Eckenrode 81

Luke M. Powers Catholic
High School
Flint, MI
Motrya Tomycz 79

Lumen Christi High School
Jackson, MI
Anonymous 13
Jerry Vogt 15
Anonymous 41

Madonna High School
Chicago, IL
Debbie Tran 72

Magnificat High School
Rocky River, OH
Adelaide Juguilon 66

Marian Catholic High School
Tamaqua, PA
Kristin Menconi 33
Jeanette Mulligan 49

Marian High School
Omaha, NE
Mary Jo Linse 28

Mary Louis Academy
Jamaica Estates, NY
Karissa Rivera 45
Tina Filiato 70

Mercy High School
Farmington Hills, MI
Maggie Kronk 55

Mount Alvernia High School
Pittsburgh, PA
Maria Muto 50

Mount de Chantal Visitation Academy
Wheeling, WV
Elizabeth Angulo 22

Nativity Parish
Fargo, ND
Kelli Schmitt 42

Niagara Catholic High School
Niagara Falls, NY
Shannon Kavanaugh 32

Notre Dame Academy
Worcester, MA
Maryellen Gruszka 29
Jennifer Bergin 62

Notre Dame–Bishop Gibbons School
Schenectady, NY
JulieAnn DeSantis 29
Suzy McEwan 41

Notre Dame High School
Batavia, NY
Teresa Griffin 17

Paramus Catholic Girls Regional High School
Paramus, NJ
Angela 17
Rosalie 60

Pomona Catholic High School
Pomona, CA
Mandy White 30
Cyndi Padilla 68

Pope John Paul II Regional High School
Boca Raton, FL
Michael McGowan 61
Stacy Sherbon 78

Presentation High School
San Jose, CA
Kristine Minione 21

Providence High School
San Antonio, TX
Bianca DeHoyos 69

Queen of Peace High School
Burbank, IL
Jennie Lonero 54

Regina High School
Harper Woods, MI
Megan Landers 47

Sacred Heart High School
Kingston, MA
Suzanne McDonald 75

Sacred Heart High School
Muenster, TX
Tony Grewing 71

86

Saint Aloysius High School
Vicksburg, MS
R. W.   46
H. M.   64

Saint Anthony High School
Wailuku, Maui, HI
Jerome Nicolas   14
Katie DeLaveaga   61

Saint Anthony's Parish
El Segundo, CA
Anonymous   19

Saint Augustine Religious
Education
Culver City, CA
Liliana Ramirez   43, 59

Saint Barbara High School
Chicago, IL
Kathleen Marie Aguinaga   42
Elvia Barrera   51

Saint Basil Academy
Philadelphia, PA
Elizabeth Mee   41

Saint Bernard High School
Playa Del Rey, CA
Keisa Johnson   62

Saint Catherine of Bologna
School
Ringwood, NJ
Randy Mc Nally   16

Saint Catherine Indian
School
Santa Fe, NM
Sean Romero   20
Halona Teba   52
Karmella Roybal   53
Leontine Earl   63
Ira Atencio   69

Saint Catherine's
High School
Racine, WI
J.C.   34

Saint Edmond High School
Fort Dodge, IA
Sarah Neppl   22

Saint Francis High School
Sacramento, CA
Dawn Davis   74

Saint Francis
Preparatory School
Fresh Meadows, NY
Olga Berwid   58

Saint Frederick High School
Monroe, LA
Daniel Moller   19
Missy Naul   24

Saint John High School
Delphos, OH
Amie Bensman   63
Janet Bockey   65

Saint John Vianney
High School
Holmdel, NJ
Matthew Flynn   20

Saint John's High School
Shrewsbury, MA
Chuck   11

Saint Joseph High School
Westchester, IL
Jamie Formanek   25
Brian Chmiel   33
Kevin McIntyre   39
Mark Wesley   49

Saint Louis Parish
Fond du Lac, WI
Senior Retreatants   44

Saint Louis School for Boys
Honolulu, HI
Mark Kubashigawa   13
Ben Yip   36

Saint Mary of the Valley
High School
Beaverton, OR
Lynn Pompili 76

Saint Mary's Academy
Milwaukee, WI
Kim LeBlanc 46

Saint Mary's High School
Sleepy Eye, MN
Jody Kuelbs 64

Saint Michael High School
New York, NY
Darlene Medina 48

Saint Michael's High School
Santa Fe, NM
Jason Bujnosek 67
Serina Lucero 77

Saint Pius V High School
Bronx, NY
Jeannie Campis 80

Saint Rose High School
Belmar, NJ
Chris Reilly 67

Saint Thomas High School
Houston, TX
Anonymous 43
Anonymous 56

Salesian High School
Richmond, CA
Anonymous 38
Anonymous 81

Santa Margarita High School
Rancho Santa Margarita, CA
Heather M. Jones 78

Stella Maris High School
Rockaway Park, NY
Lisa Solis 68

Thomas More Prep–Marian
Hays, KS
Kelly Cox 23
Terra Ryan 25

Towson Catholic
High School
Towson, MD
Ann Pilon 19
Kim Brock 52

Villa Maria Academy
Buffalo, NY
Jennifer Cassell 38
Amy Weber 57
Virginia C. Rishkofski 80